KIDZ BOP SONGBOOK

ISBN 978-1-4584-0302-5

HAL•LEONARD®
CORPORATION

7777 W. BLUEMOUND RD. P.O. BOX 13819 MILWAUKEE, WI 53213

Visit Hal Leonard Online at
www.halleonard.com

AIRPLANES

Words and Music by BOBBY RAY SIMMONS JR.,
ALEXANDER GRANT, JEREMY DUSSOLLIETY,
TIM SOMMERS and JUSTIN FRANKS

Can we pre-tend that air - planes _ in the night sky _ are like shoot-in' stars? _ I could real-ly use a

Additional Lyrics

Rap 1:   Yeah, I could use a dream or a genie or a wish to go back to a place much simpler than this.
'Cause after all the partyin' and smashin' and crashin', and all the glitz and the glam and the fashion,
And all the pandemonium and all the madness, there comes a time where you fade to the blackness.
And when you starin' at that phone in your lap, and you hopin', but them people never call you back.
But that's just how the story unfolds, you get another hand soon after you fold.
And when your plans unravel in the sand, what would you wish for if you had one chance?
So, airplane, airplane, sorry I'm late. I'm on my way, so don't close that gate.
If I don't make that then I'll switch my flight and I'll be right back at it by the end of the night.
Chorus

Rap 2:   Yeah, yeah, somebody take me back to the days before this was a job, before I got paid.
Before it ever mattered what I had in my bank, yeah, back when I was tryin' to get a tip at Subway.
And back when I was rappin' for the thrill of it, but now-a-days we rappin' to stay relevant.
I'm guessin' that if we can make some wishes outta airplanes, then maybe, yo, maybe I'll go back to the days
Before the politics that we call the rap game, and back when ain't nobody listen to my mix tape,
And back before I tried to cover up my slang. But this is for Decatur, what's up Bobby Ray?
So can I get a wish to end the politics and get back to the music that started this hit?
So here I stand, and then again I say I'm hopin' we can make some wishes outta airplanes.
Chorus

ANIMAL

Words and Music by TIM PAGNOTTA,
TYLER GLENN, BRANDEN CAMPBELL,
ELAINE DOTY and CHRISTOPHER ALLEN

BABY

Words and Music by JUSTIN BIEBER,
CHRISTOPHER STEWART, CHRISTINE FLORES,
CHRISTOPHER BRIDGES and TERIUS NASH

With energy

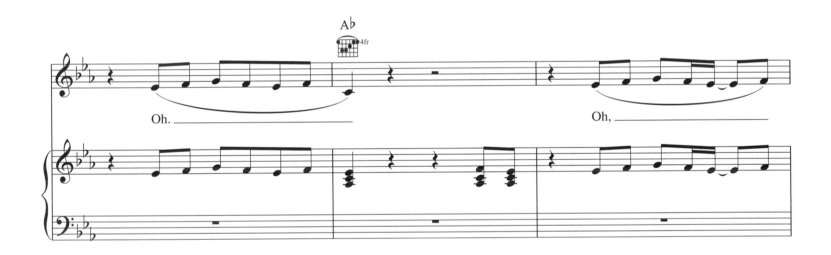

BAD DAY

Words and Music by
DANIEL POWTER

DYNAMITE

Words and Music by TAIO CRUZ,
LUKASZ GOTTWALD, MAX MARTIN,
BENJAMIN LEVIN and BONNIE McKEE

Moderate Dance groove

BILLIONAIRE

Words and Music by TRAVIS McCOY,
PHILIP LAWRENCE, BRUNO MARS
and ARI LEVINE

Moderate Reggae feel

I wan-na be a bil-lion-aire __ so ver-y bad, __ buy all of the things I nev-er had.

I wan-na be on the cov-er of

oh, _____ oh, _____ when I'm ___

___ a bil - lion - aire, ___ oh, _____ oh. ___

___ I want to be a

bil - lion - aire ___ so ver - y bad. ___

rall.

BREAK YOUR HEART

Words and Music by TAIO CRUZ,
CHRISTOPHER BRIDGES and FRASER T. SMITH

D.S. al Coda

Eh, told you from the start, _____ eh, I'm on-ly gon-na

heart. ___ Whoa, _____ whoa. ___

Whoa,

whoa.

CAN'T BUY ME LOVE

Words and Music by JOHN LENNON
and PAUL McCARTNEY

Can't buy me love, _____ oh, _____ love _

_____ oh, _____ can't buy me love, _____ oh. _____ I'll

buy you a dia-mond ring, ___ my friend, if it makes you feel al-right,
give you ___ all I've got ___ to give _ if you say you love me too, ___

Instrumental solo

COOLER THAN ME

Words and Music by MIKE POSNER
and ERIC HOLLJES

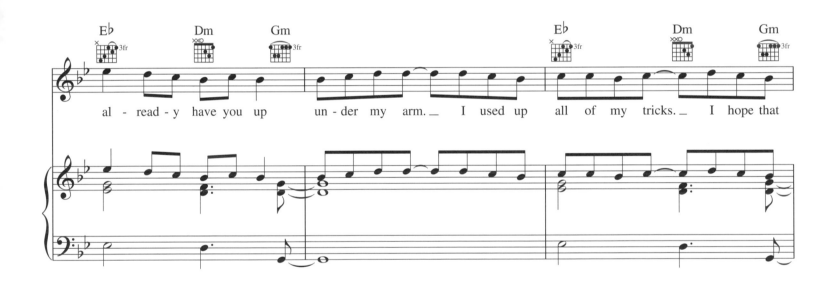

sign - er shades __ just to hide your face __ and you wear 'em a - round __ like you're

cool - er than me. __ And you nev - er say hey __ or re - mem - ber my name, __ and it's

prob - a - bly 'cause __ you think you're cool - er than me. __

Play 3 times

N.C.

prob - a - bly 'cause ___ you think you're cool - er than me. ___

FIFTEEN

Words and Music by
TAYLOR SWIFT

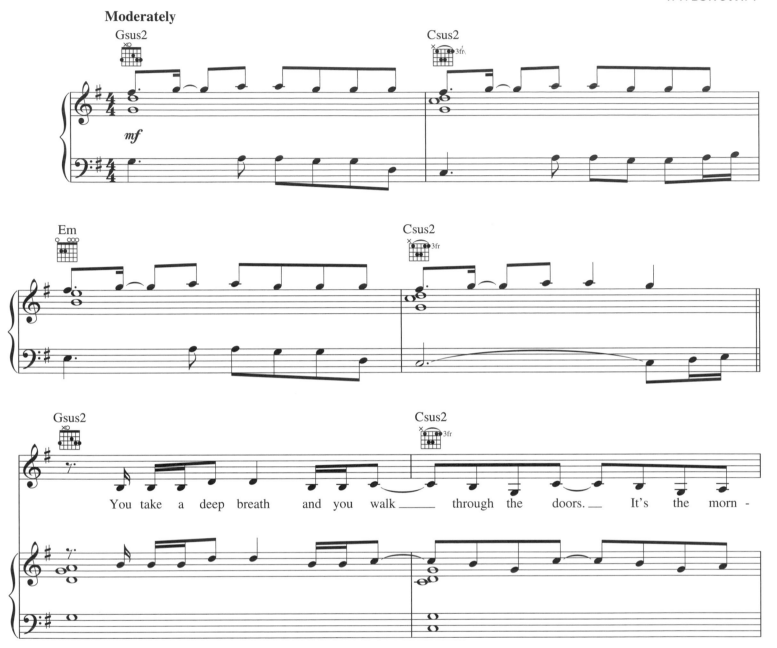

JUST THE WAY YOU ARE

Words and Music by BRUNO MARS,
ARI LEVINE, PHILIP LAWRENCE,
KHARI CAIN and KHALIL WALTON

Moderate Hip-Hop groove

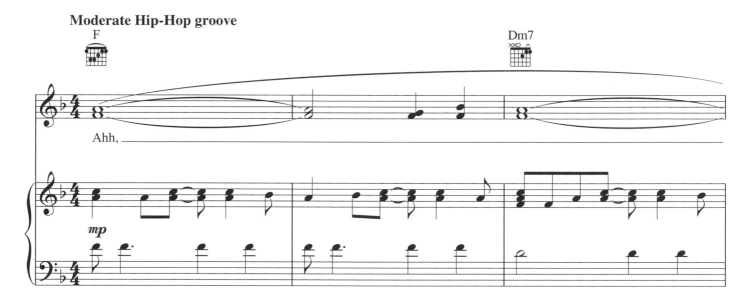

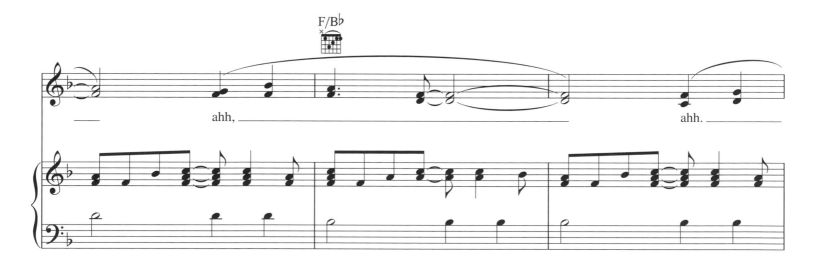

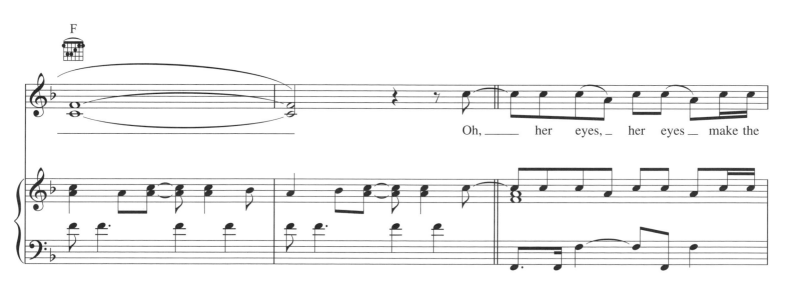

But ev-'ry time __ she asks __ me, "Do __ I look __ o - kay?" __ I __ say: __

When I see your face, __ there's not a thing __ that I __ would change, __

'cause you're a - maz - ing __ just __ the way __ you are. __

And when you smile, __

CODA

The way — you are, — the way — you are. —

Dm7   F/B♭

— Girl, you're a-maz - ing ——— just —

F

— the way — you are. — When I see your face, —

Dm7

there's not a thing — that I — would change, — 'cause you're a-maz -

FIREWORK

Words and Music by MIKKEL ERIKSEN,
TOR ERIK HERMANSEN, ESTHER DEAN,
KATY PERRY and SANDY WILHELM

HEY, SOUL SISTER

Words and Music by PAT MONAHAN,
ESPEN LIND and AMUND BJORKLAND

Moderately

Hey, ____ hey, _____ hey! _____

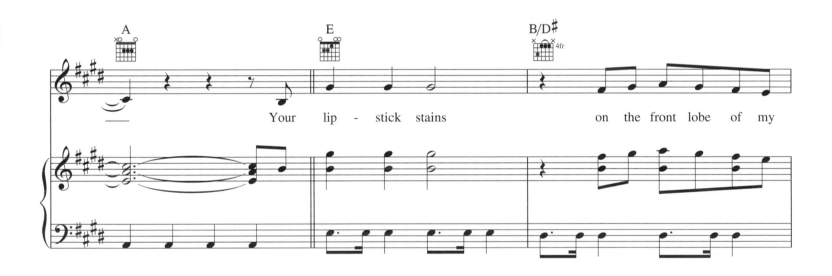

Your lip - stick stains _____ on the front lobe of my

left - side brains. I knew ____ I would - n't for - get ya, and so I went and

I GOTTA FEELING

Words and Music by WILL ADAMS,
ALLAN PINEDA, JAIME GOMEZ,
STACY FERGUSON, DAVID GUETTA
and FREDERIC RIESTERER

I got-ta feel-

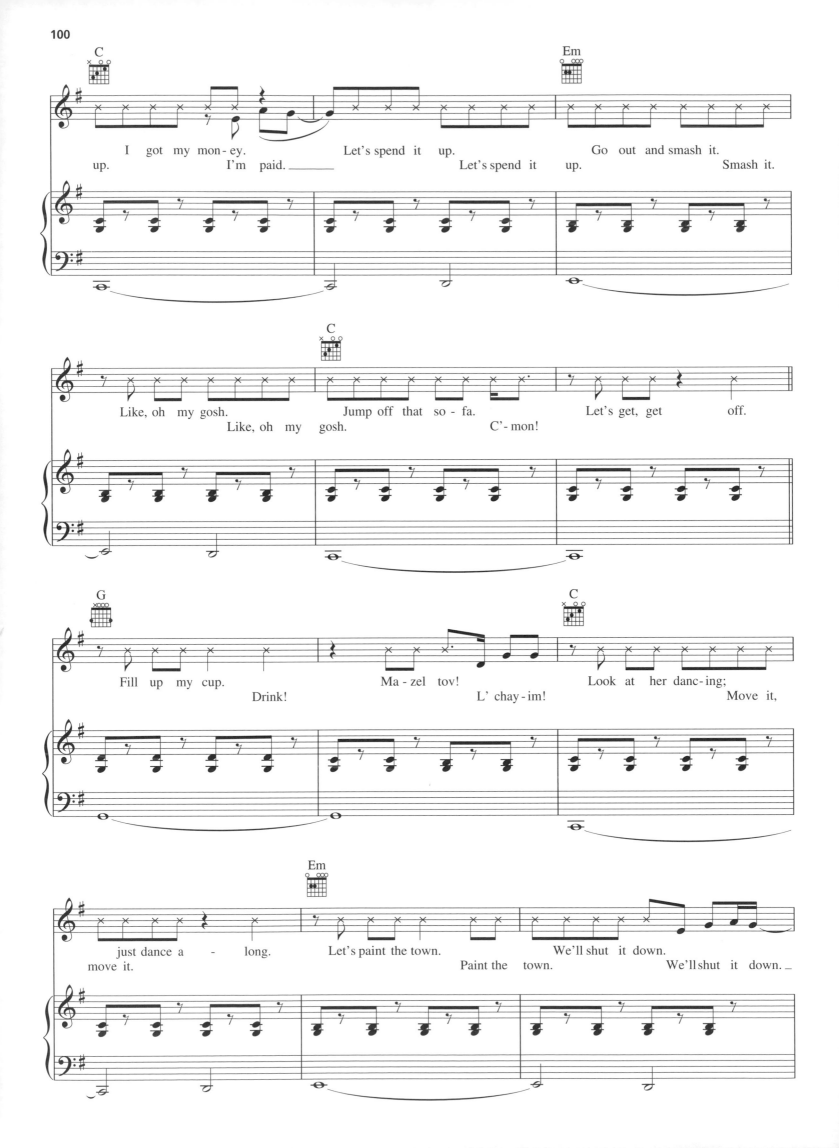

IF I HAD YOU

Words and Music by SAVAN KOTECHA,
JOHAN SCHUSTER and MAX MARTIN

MAGIC

Words and Music by BOBBY SIMMONS, JR.,
LUKASZ GOTTWALD and RIVERS CUOMO

* Recorded a half step higher.

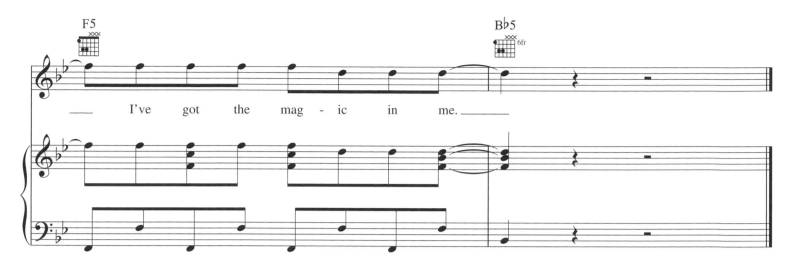

I've got the mag - ic in me.

Additional Lyrics

Rap 1: These tricks that I'll attempt will blow your mind.
Pick a verse, any verse, I'll hypnotise you wit' every line.
I'll need a volunteer. How 'bout you, with the eyes?
Come on down to the front, and stand right here and don't be shy.
I have you time travelin', have your mind babblin'.
People try'n a inherit the skill so they askin' me.
Even David Blaine had to go and take some classes, and
I see Mindfreak like, "What's up, man? What's happenin'?"
So come one, come all, and see the show tonight.
Prepare to be astounded, no ghost or poltergeist.
You know I'm no Pinocchio, I never told a lie.
So call me Mr. Magic Man, I float on Cloud 9.

Rap 2: Well, take a journey into my mind, you'll see why it's venom I rhyme.
Stay on the road, so I call my mama when I got time.
I hit the stage, go insane, then jump into that crowd.
See, see, when I rhyme I flow on the beat like Pidda-da-da.
See, I deceive you with my intergalactic ether.
I sing just like Aretha, so respect me like I'm Caesar.
I kick it like Adidas, well, only sticky like adhesive.
Be cautious, 'cause what I be on'll leave you with amnesia.
I break all the rules like Evel Knievel.
It's a spectacular show, 'cause my heart pumps diesel.
So whatever you sayin', it don't entertain my ego.
I do this every day, hocus pocus is my steelo.

PARTY IN THE U.S.A.

Words and Music by JESSICA CORNISH,
LUKASZ GOTTWALD and CLAUDE KELLY

Moderate Pop

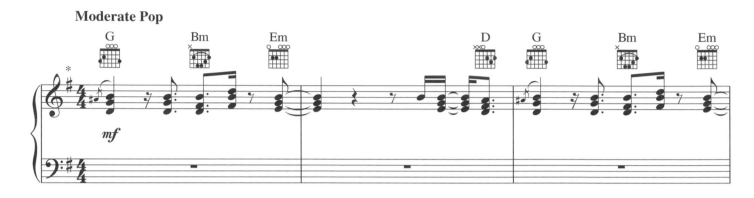

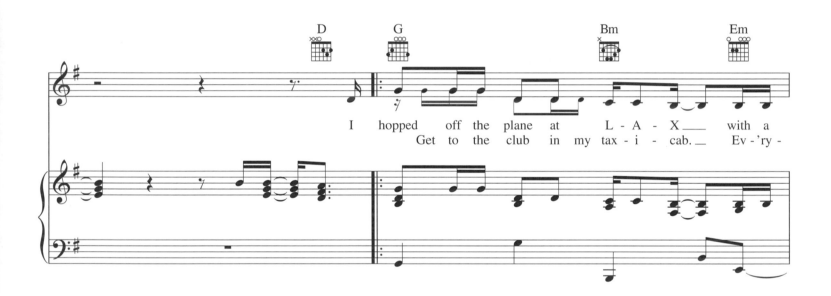

I hopped off the plane at L-A-X___ with a
Get to the club in my tax-i-cab.___ Ev-'ry-

dream and my car-di-gan.___ Wel-come to the land of fame, ex-cess.___
bod-y's look-in' at me now,___ like, "Who's that chick that's rock-in' kicks?___ She's

* Recorded a half step lower.

LET IT BE

Words and Music by JOHN LENNON
and PAUL McCARTNEY

When I find my-self __ in times of trou-ble
Instrumental

Moth-er Mar - y comes to me speak-ing words of wis-dom; let it

be. __ And in my hour of dark - ness, she is